50 FACTS ABOUT ANIMALS

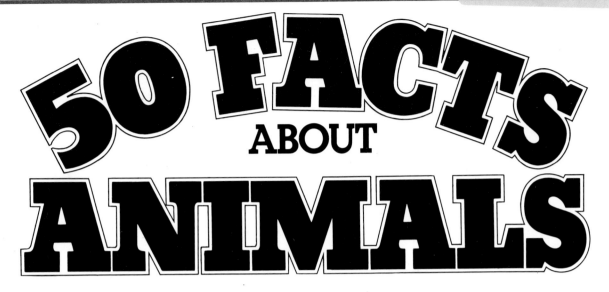

by
Ron Taylor

Sara-Jane Adams

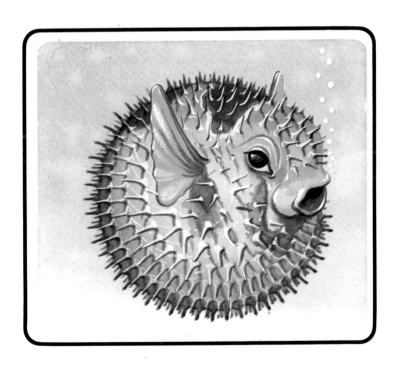

A Piccolo Explorer Book

CONTENTS

Why do wood-peckers peck?

This green woodpecker is about to start pecking into the bark of the tree with his strong, sharp bill (beak). While out walking, you may have heard the very rapid rat-tat-tat that tells you that a woodpecker is pecking a tree in a nearby wood.

Woodpeckers peck for three main reasons. First of all, they make their nests inside the trunks of trees. For this, they have to drill out a large hole with their beaks. Both the cock and the hen woodpecker help to make the nest in this way.

Secondly, woodpeckers feed on insects and insect larvae (grubs) that live in bark and wood. They quickly drill a small hole, then lick up the insect with their long tongue.

Finally, in spring, woodpeckers peck rapidly at hard, dead wood to make a loud drumming sound that will attract a mate.

Which dogs live in tunnels?

Prairie dogs look like giant hamsters but are more closely related to squirrels. They are called 'dogs' because of the sound of their barking calls. They live in the North American plains, in 'towns' made up of hundreds of kilometres of underground tunnels. Like our towns, those of prairie dogs have different districts. Those that live in one district are suspicious of prairie dogs from other districts, just as people were once wary of other people from different villages.

Prairie dogs pile up mounds of soil around the entrance holes to their burrows. Then a prairie watchdog keeps watch from the mound for strangers coming over the plains. If a stranger does come, the watchdog quickly vanishes down the hole to warn other members of the family. When the stranger is another prairie dog, the watchdog rushes out, barking, to drive it off. But if, after all, it is only another member of the family, then the watchdog will go up to it and greet it in the way shown in the picture.

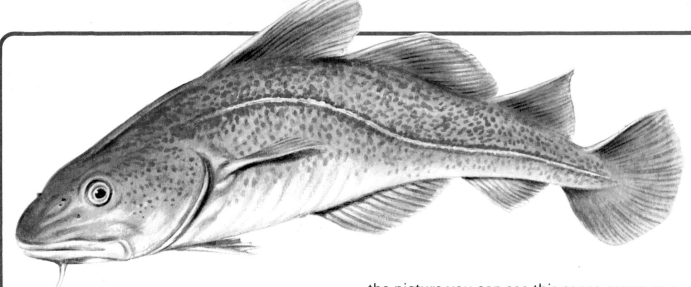

3 What special sense do fishes have?

Like other animals, fishes rely on their sense organs for all their life activities, such as finding their way about and catching food. But fishes have one sense organ that no land animal has. This is called the 'lateral line'. In the picture you can see this sense organ as a distinct line running along the side of this cod. It also has one on its other side.

The lateral line is really a long groove which contains many nerve endings. These feel changes in the water pressure, which helps the fish to tell how far away objects are. This sense is very important for fishes that swim in large shoals (groups). It allows each fish to sense how far away other fishes are and to keep far enough away from the others to avoid bumping into them.

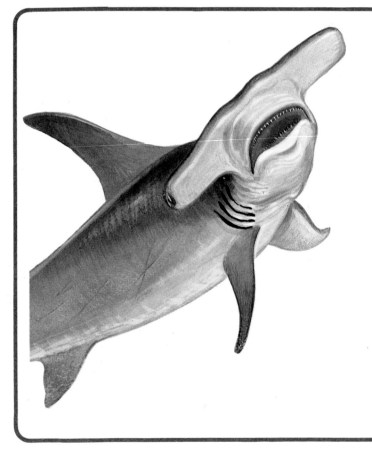

4 Which fish has a hammer head?

The fish in the picture is a fierce shark. No prizes will be given for guessing why it is called the hammerhead shark. You can see that its eyes are on the very outside ends of the 'hammer'. Its nostrils lie just behind the eyes, also on the very outside of the head. Its mouth, curving in a wicked gape, lies on the underside, just where the 'handle' of the body meets the 'hammer' of the head. The rest of the shark's body is fairly normally shark-shaped. So why does this shark have such a peculiarly-shaped head?

The truth is that no one is sure. Some animal experts think that the distance between the eyes and nostrils may help the hammerhead to pinpoint its prey. But other sharks get on very well without a hammer head!

5   **Where do turtles lay their eggs?**

Out of the depths of the tropical ocean the green turtles come to lay their eggs on land. Each mother turtle heaves herself slowly up the beach, scoops out a nest hole in the sand and lays her eggs. Then, without ever waiting to see her offspring, she goes back to her lonely ocean life.

As the hatchlings break out of their eggs they must race for the safety of the sea in order to survive. Most of the little turtles will never reach the sea. They will be snapped up by hungry predators such as seabirds and lizards who lie in wait for them.

6   **How far does an eel travel?**

The life of the river eel is one long, fantastic journey. As adults, the eels leave their home rivers and swim thousands of kilometres to their breeding grounds in the far Sargasso Sea, in the middle of the Atlantic Ocean. The journey back for the young eels, or elvers, is still more amazing. These tiny, leaf-like creatures gradually change into adult eels as they swim for as long as three years to reach their home rivers – the very same rivers their parents set out from.

When do chicks peck their parents?

When we need to tell someone something we use words. Birds use special calls or cries, which are rather like words. But birds also speak to each other through what are called displays. These are special body movements or the showing of special body patterns. Each display has a particular meaning to other birds.

In the picture, the parent herring gull has landed on the nest with food in its crop – a pouch in its gullet. As it lands it displays a red spot on its bill to the chick. When the chick sees the red spot it pecks it, telling the parent bird to let go of the food.

8 Which bird walks on water?

If you ever go walking in marshy country and you suddenly hear terrible groans and squeals coming from the reeds, this is probably not someone dying, but a water rail calling from its nest. This small marsh bird is much more often heard than seen, and has a variety of calls. These include cluckings and cat-like miaowings, and also a loud groaning, squealing call which is particularly scary at night!

If you find the water rail, you may think it looks funny rather than sinister. Like a moorhen, only a little smaller, it is a brownish bird with a long red beak and rather absurdly long, narrow toes. These, however, are very useful for keeping the water rail from sinking into the marshes. The water rail's body is narrow, which probably helps it to squeeze through crowded marsh stems. You would think that its big feet would then get in the way, but as you can see from the picture, the rail can fold its feet into a narrow shape.

9 Which bird sounds like a foghorn?

There can be only one answer to this question – a bittern. This marsh bird has one of the most low-pitched of all bird calls. It reminds people more of a ship's foghorn than of familiar birdsong.

Bitterns are like herons but have shorter necks. A parent bittern is usually to be found deep among the marsh reeds, guarding its nestlings. If you find it there it will rear up its head and beak in the way shown here. This is really to get a better look at you, because the bittern's eyes are set low down behind its thick bill.

10 Which birds will share a nest?

Sometimes fierce, flesh-eating animals will live together with smaller, more defenceless animals without trying to do them any harm. You may have a cat in your house that has stopped trying to get at your pet birds because it has got used to them.

Pet birds are usually safe inside their cages anyway, and the cat has just lost interest in them because it knows that the chase is useless. In nature, however, there are no protective cages. Yet here too, fierce and defenceless animals can sometimes be found living together peacefully.

The picture shows one good example. Here, a fierce golden eagle and a much smaller, more defenceless starling are sharing a rocky ledge. Both have their nests there. In fact the dauntless starling has actually built its nest inside that of the great bird of prey. Yet the starling and eagle families continue to live in peace. Or rather, like the cat and birds, they simply ignore one another. Of course, if the winter should be hard, so that rabbits are scarce . . .

11 Why do caribou like the snow?

Caribou, the reindeer of North America, migrate northwards in the less cold months when the snow begins to melt over their harsh northern homelands, or territory. But usually, even though many parts of their territory are now free of snow, so that the tasty mosses and grasses are easier to get at, the caribou stick to travelling and feeding on the snow-covered areas. Here, they have to paw away the snow to get at their green food.

This would seem very puzzling at first, until you think of what is happening in the swampy, melted areas, where countless millions of flies and other Arctic summer pests are hatching every day!

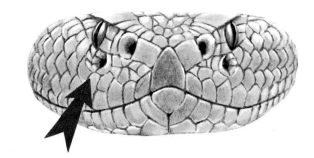

12 How did pit vipers get their name?

Pit vipers are very venomous, or poisonous, snakes that live in warm parts of the world. Examples are the cottonmouth and the bushmaster of America and the deadly fer-de-lance of the West Indies. Pit vipers have a sixth sense, by which they can find their prey even in the dark. This is a *heat* sense. The hollows, or pits, under a pit viper's eyes are sense organs that pick up heat from the body of any small mammal that is nearby. This type of warm-blooded creature is the pit viper's favourite prey.

13 How big are a fox's ears?

We know the fox as a reddish, dog-like creature that is chased by huntsmen and often robs our town dustbins. But several more kinds of foxes live in other parts of the world. These can often be recognized by the size of their ears, depending on whether the fox lives in hot or cold lands.

Our own common fox lives in a temperate country and has medium-sized ears. The Arctic fox has much smaller ears. This is sensible because large ears give off more heat and that is the last thing an Arctic animal wants to do. On the other hand, desert animals often do want to lose heat, so the desert fox has big ears.

Arctic fox　　　　**Desert fox**

14 Do honeybees go shopping?

In a way they do, because they take their 'shopping baskets' with them. These are parts of a bee's hind legs. They are used for carrying pollen, which is one of the bee's foods that it takes from flowers. The other food is nectar, from which it makes honey. Pollen is the powdery stuff found on the anthers, or male parts, of flowers. When a bee visits a flower the pollen falls all over the bee's body. The bee then brushes this pollen into its pollen baskets using the 'brushes' and 'combs' that are the spiky parts of its legs. Pollen is used by the bee to make bee bread.

15 When is an ant a lion?

Adult ant-lions are rather like small, delicate dragonflies. They are completely different from the larvae, or young insects, which are large and wingless and have enormous, pincer-like poison jaws. Ant-lion larvae are, for their size, much more ferocious than lions themselves, but these little creatures are less than a centimetre long.

Not only is the ant-lion larva fiercely armed, but it also makes a clever trap for catching its prey of ants and spiders. After digging out the trap from sandy soil it waits at the bottom, jaws at the ready. When an insect comes near the edge of the trap, the ant-lion throws sand at it and the insect falls in.

16 Where do ants live?

Woodland ants build large and elaborate nests using materials such as pine needles and chewed wood. Other common ants build equally roomy nests underground in the soil. When you disturb an ant nest, or colony, the ants will run about in a rather aimless way. But in fact, ant colonies are very well organized.

An ant colony is begun by one or more queen ants. From a queen ant's eggs are born all the other ants of the colony. (The king or male ants have died off.) Most of these ants are the worker ants you see scurrying about. In the picture you can see workers tending aphids. These are plant insects that give the ants a sweet juice.

17 Which fish can blow itself up?

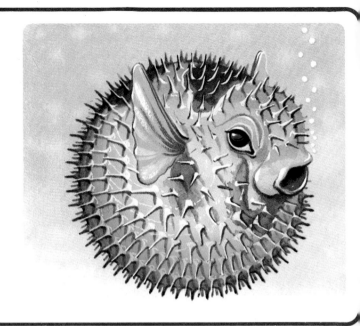

The porcupine fish, like its close relative the puffer fish, defends itself by changing its shape. When threatened, these little tropical fishes draw water into their bodies, causing them to swell up into a hard ball. In this way the porcupine fish makes its spiny body a really prickly mouthful for any larger fish that tries to swallow it. When the danger has passed, the porcupine fish squirts the water out from its body and goes back to its fairly ordinary fishy shape.

18 What hums, flies and drinks nectar?

One correct answer would be a bee, but in this case it is a hummingbird. These tiny, colourful birds live in tropical countries and get their food mostly from flowers. The picture shows a velvet purple coronet hummingbird feeding from a hibiscus flower. It is sucking up the flower's nectar through its long, tubular tongue. As it hovers motionless by the flower its wings beat so fast that they make a humming noise.

19 Which animal is the biggest ever?

The answer is a blue whale and it is an animal that lives today, although its numbers have been tragically reduced by hunting. This vast creature, which is a mammal like ourselves, grows up to more than 30 metres long and weighs up to 140 tonnes. It is as long as four large motor coaches end to end and as heavy as 30 elephants! Despite its huge size, the blue whale feeds on shrimp-like krill, four centimetres long.

Graham Allen

20 Do penguins make nests?

The Adélie penguins in the picture live, like various other types of penguins, in the cold world of the Antarctic. In the short Antarctic summer during December some of the snow melts, exposing bare, pebble-strewn soil.

The male penguin then collects pebbles and drops them, as offerings, at the feet of his chosen mate. Eventually she accepts, and arranges the pebbles around her to make the Adélie's simple nest.

21 What can eat a hedgehog?

The answer is a badger. The hedgehog in the picture is in great danger with badgers only a tuft of grass away. If attacked, the hedgehog would immediately roll itself up into a prickly ball. This might keep away a cat or a fox, but not a badger. With its tough mouth, strong jaws and long, sharp teeth, the badger would make short work of even the prickliest hedgehog. The picture shows the animals at night. Badgers and hedgehogs are both nocturnal. This means that they come out to feed mostly at night and are rarely seen during the daytime.

22 Where does a bumblebee nest?

You probably know that honeybees nest either in hives made by people, or in large papery nests usually found in bushes or trees. But where do bumblebees, live? The answer used to be in many country corners such as hedgerows, banksides and the eaves of thatched cottages. But thatched cottages are rarer than they once were and many hedges, alas, have been grubbed up by farmers anxious to grow more crops. Most bumblebees nowadays nest underground.

A favourite nesting site of the queen bumblebee is an old mousehole. This not only offers protection for her young, but may even contain some dry grass left from the mouse nest, which she can use as a place to lay her eggs. Unlike the honeybees' nest, which contains thousands of bees and eggs, the bumblebees' nest has only a few hundred. Usually, the colony last only until the winter.

23 Does a flamingo have any relatives?

A flamingo is a peculiar bird with stilt-like legs and an equally long neck. It feeds in water with its head upside-down. It does not look very much like any other bird, so does it have any close relatives? Ornithologists (bird experts) think that there are two types of birds that might be related to the flamingo, but they can't decide which is the right one.

Young flamingos look and fly rather like storks, so flamingos may be related to the stork family. But all birds have small insects, called lice, which live among their feathers and these give a clue in another direction. The feather lice of flamingos look more like those of ducks, geese and swans than those of storks, so the nearest relatives of flamingos may be the goose family.

24 What animal is called a joey?

You may know already that this is the name given to a young kangaroo while it is still living in its mother's roomy pouch. When very young, the joey spends all its time there, sucking milk from the teats inside the pouch. But how it gets to the pouch in the first place is a truly amazing story.

Although the mother kangaroo may be as tall as a man and much heavier, her newborn baby is a tiny creature no bigger than a bean. It is naked and blind, because neither its hair nor its eyes are yet developed. In fact, the newborn kangaroo is at about the same stage of development as a human baby six months *before* birth.

Yet after its birth this tiny, half-formed creature makes its own way from its mother's birth canal to her pouch. It drags itself slowly along the fur of her belly using the claws of its more developed front legs, until it reaches the safety of the pouch. Here it seizes a teat with its mouth and stays plugged-on until it has grown enormously. Even then, as you can see, the mother's pouch remains the joey's home for quite a long time.

25 What has hair and lays eggs?

There are just two answers to this question – a platypus and an echidna. These are the only mammals, or animals with hair, that lay eggs. These two types of mammal are leftovers from very ancient mammals that lived 200 million years ago, long before the mammals we know today had appeared.

They have other peculiarities too. Whereas all other mammals feed their young from milk glands which have teats, the platypus and echidna feed their hatchlings with milk that oozes from slits.

Both the platypus and the echidna come from Australasia. The platypus is a strange-looking creature with the beak and webbed feet of a duck and the broad, flat tail of a beaver. The echidna, shown below, looks even more peculiar. It has long spines sticking through its fur, a long, thin nose and a big-footed, waddling gait.

Spiny echidna

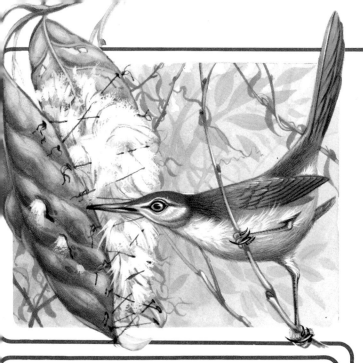

26 Which bird can sew?

Tailor birds live in warm south-eastern countries. They are small, not very noticeable birds and are related to warblers. They get their name from their clever habit of stitching leaves together to make a neat nest for their chicks. They start doing this by punching holes in the edges of two leaves with their sharp, pointed beaks. Then, pulling the leaves together, they thread small lengths of tough fibre through the holes. Next, the tailor birds fray out the ends of the fibre lengths. This stops the fibres from slipping back through the holes and letting the leaves loose. Finally, the birds line the leafy pouch with soft grasses or fibres to make a cosy nest.

27 What is a lizard's secret weapon?

The frilled lizard of Australia is about one metre long, has very small teeth and can harm nothing much bigger than the insects on which it feeds. Perhaps it is because of this harmlessness that the lizard has a remarkable way of defending itself.

   This is the large, brightly coloured frill that it can raise suddenly all around its head. Usually it does this only when cornered and frightened by an enemy. At the same time, it gapes open its mouth very wide then gives a sharp hiss. Although this is all show, it can scare off even a much larger, better-armed enemy such as a dingo or some other aggressive dog.

28 What can a kiwi do best?

The kiwi is a flightless bird of New Zealand and it is remarkable in many ways. Although only as big as a rooster, it lays very large eggs, about $12\frac{1}{2}$ centimetres long. Its feathers look more like hair than the feathers of other birds. It has small eyes, but a better sense of smell than any other living bird. Its nostrils are on the end of its beak and this helps it to find its food of grubs deep down in the soil.

29 Where can you find wolves and devils?

Before Europeans came to Australia, the four-legged animals there nearly all belonged to the kangaroo and koala family. That is, they were almost all pouched mammals (marsupials). Nowadays, Australia swarms with rabbits, cats and dogs as well as sheep and cattle.

Although Australia is a very big place, these imported animals have not done the native marsupials much good. Kangaroos and other animals have been heavily hunted. Some marsupials have become so rare that they are extinct in Australia itself, and are only rarely seen in the neighbouring island of Tasmania. The Tasmanian wolf, the biggest marsupial flesh-eater, may now be extinct there, too. But the equally ferocious Tasmanian devil still survives.

Tasmanian devil

Tasmanian wolf

30 Which owl lives in a cactus?

Owls are birds of prey that fly at dusk or at night. Their feathers are especially soft, making them the most silent of birds in flight, and allowing them to glide down noiselessly on some unsuspecting prey. An owl can see its prey in the dark by means of the keen night vision of its large eyes.

Altogether, about 135 different kinds, or species, of owl haunt the night in various parts of the world. Many of these owls live in trees or, as in the case of the barn owl, in the roof spaces of buildings.

Some other owls live in burrows. Among these is the burrowing owl of the North American prairies. This small owl often takes over burrows left vacant by other plains animals, such as the prairie dogs shown on page 3. Another small owl, the elf owl, lives in burrowed-out holes in giant desert cactuses, like the one shown here.

31 Which frog builds a nursery?

The numerous little frogs called tree frogs are not altogether well named. Although many of them do, in fact, live all their lives in trees, many other tree frogs spend most or all of their time elsewhere. Some tree frogs live mostly in water, others make their homes in mud burrows, and a few have taken to living in people's houses, where they are useful fly catchers.

Tree frogs are spread widely throughout the warmer, wetter parts of the world. Among South American tree frogs is the smith frog, which builds a home of mud, shaped like a circular stockade.

But this stockade is really more like a nursery. This is where the female smith frog lays her eggs and where her tadpoles can hatch, swim around and feed on plants, all with a certain amount of extra safety from their enemies. To make the nursery, the male frog piles up mud then smooths it with his forelegs to the required shape.

32 What has scales and eats ants?

The answer to this question – a pangolin – puzzled scientists for many centuries. The Romans, for example, thought that the pangolin was a sort of small crocodile. Not a bad guess, because the pangolin's body is long-tailed and is covered all over with hard scales. However, the Romans were wrong. The pangolin, despite its scaliness, is a warm-blooded mammal. It has no teeth and lives on ants and termites, which it licks up with its long tongue. When scared or sleepy, it curls up like this into a scaly ball.

33 Where do horses swim with lions?

Zebra fish

Lion fish

Sea horse

The answer is in the sea. In the picture a gaudy, spiny lion fish swims together with a couple of sea horses, which look like knights from some underwater chess game. Also in this watery zoo, but swimming out of the picture, is a zebra fish.

You may think that the sea horse and the zebra fish are well named, but that the lion fish looks nothing like a lion. Well, it has another, more appropriate name – scorpion fish. Among those brilliantly coloured spines are some that deliver a very painful sting.

34 Which creatures carry lamps?

In the inky mid-depths of the ocean, about one to several kilometres down, live some very strange creatures that carry their own lamps and fishing lines with them. Shown in the picture are, from top to bottom: a luminous squid; a female anglerfish with two luminous lures; a stomiatoid fish with a long, bright lure; a brightly glowing hatchet fish, and at the bottom, another stomiatoid fish with lamp-like spots on its face.

Why do many of these fishes have brightly-shining lures? The answer is that they need them to attract the attention of smaller creatures, which mistake the lures for their own even smaller, luminous prey. The fishes have big mouths because their meals come by so rarely they can't afford to miss them!

35 Which bird wears three coats a year?

Many birds change their plumage from a winter to a summer coat, and vice versa. The ptarmigan, however, goes one better and has three changes of coat in the year. Ptarmigan (pronounced tarmigan, and it is the same for more than one) are a sort of grouse, similar in many ways to the birds that are shot in huge numbers on moors for huge amounts of money.

Like the moor grouse, ptarmigan are plumpish birds about 35 centimetres long when fully grown. In the winter, both cock and hen ptarmigan are white nearly all over. In the spring, the cock turns a mottled brownish-yellow, and the hen a lighter yellow colour. Both keep their white bellies. In the autumn, they change their camouflage for the third time, when they both become a more greyish colour, before turning white again for winter.

36 Why does a crossbill's beak cross?

The crossbill is a rather colourful finch that lives in northern places all around the world. Its most remarkable feature is its large, sharp-pointed bill, which unlike any other finch's bill, crosses over at the tip.

Although it may look a bit awkward, the crossed bill is, in fact, a perfect tool for opening the scales of pine cones. One twist with the bill, and the crossbill's tongue can pull out a tasty seed.

37 What hatches eggs in its mouth?

Mouth breeders are various kinds of small fishes, some of which live in rivers or lakes, and others in the sea. Among them are some catfishes and many jawfishes and cardinal fishes. Parent mouth breeders use their mouths as a hatchery and nursery for their young. More often it is the father of the brood who takes the eggs into his mouth soon after he has fertilized them with his spawn. There, he protects the eggs from being snapped up as food by other fishes (including, sometimes, the mother!) and also provides the eggs with airy water fanned from his gills.

When the young fishes (the fry) hatch, the father still keeps watch over them and if danger threatens he takes them back into his mouth for protection. In some cardinal fishes, no fewer than 20,000 eggs and fry may be hatched and nursed in this way.

38 How does a musk ox defend itself?

Musk oxen look like highland cattle, but they are really more closely related to sheep and goats. They live in the snow-bound regions of northern Canada and Greenland. Their long, shaggy coats are so warm that they do not have to take shelter even during the intensely cold Arctic winter. They remain wherever their food of grasses and mosses is most plentiful.

Wolves are known to attack musk oxen, but often without much success. The large musk oxen form a tight ring with their young in the middle and use their sharp horns to protect themselves. Unfortunately, this same defence is worse than useless against human hunters, because it makes the musk-ox group into a standing target. The musk ox gets its name from the musk glands on the face of the male, which give off a strong, musky smell.

39 What lives in tubes in muddy shores?

Muddy or sandy seashores are home for many different kinds of animals, from large ones such as seals to medium-sized wading birds, to crabs, starfishes and other creatures.

Many small burrowing creatures make their homes actually below the mud or sand. Six of them are shown in the picture. The otter shell, razor shell, tellin and cockle are all molluscs, relatives of snails and octopuses. The parchment worm is a tube-dwelling relative of the earthworm and of the sea-dwelling annelid worms. The sea cucumber is a relative of the starfish. These are only a few of the host of different animals that have taken to a life beneath the shore.

40 How do barracudas keep clean?

The little blue fish inside the fearsome jaws of the barracuda is a cleaner fish. It is quite safe there, despite the barracuda's ability to make a meal of much larger fishes. What protects the cleaner fish? The answer seems to be that the barracuda recognizes the little cleaner as a helper, who will clear away the parasites and bits of loose skin inside the barracuda's mouth. The cleaner fish, on the other hand, regards all these as tasty titbits. The other little blue fish is called a false cleaner. It looks so like a cleaner that it also is safe from the barracuda – but it does no cleaning!

41 When is a frog not a frog?

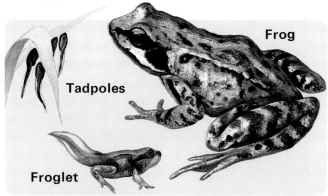

Frog

Tadpoles

Froglet

The answer is when it is a tadpole. Tadpoles hatch from a frog's eggs and live underwater, breathing air with the aid of their gills, as fishes do. The adult frog has no gills and breathes air mostly through its skin and sometimes, as with this common frog, also with the use of its lungs. The great change that happens, which turns a water-breathing tadpole into an air-breathing frog, is called metamorphosis.

Metamorphosis is controlled by a tadpole's thyroid gland. If this gland takes in iodine, metamorphosis happens early and produces a tiny frog. If the thyroid gland is removed, metamorphosis never happens and the tadpole just goes on growing!

42 What uses its ears as fans?

Many animals use their ears to lose heat from their bodies. In this case, the best answer to the question would be an African elephant because its great ears are certainly the most fan-like in the animal world. They are larger even than those of its close relative, the Indian elephant, which also lives in a hot country but stays more in the shade. Both these huge beasts, which are the largest of living land animals (the African elephant being the bigger) also cool themselves by wallowing in water and spraying water over their bodies with their trunks.

43 Which moth was changed by smoke?

A hundred and fifty years ago, the peppered moth was a common, speckled-whitish insect found in the English countryside. But at this time, many parts of the country were becoming blackened by clouds of smoke from the new factories.

Every now and then, a darker-coloured peppered moth would be born. Previously, such a moth would have been easily seen against a tree trunk and would be picked off by hungry birds more often than the normal, whitish variety. But now, on the soot-darkened tree trunks, the darker-coloured variety was the less easily seen, and so it was the lighter-coloured moths that got picked off.

Eventually, in industrial areas, the darker-coloured moths became the normal ones because more of them survived, and because they had dark-coloured offspring. The lighter-coloured peppered moths, on the other hand, became very rare. This change in an animal species is called evolution.

44 What turns into a butterfly?

Butterflies go through a number of life stages, in which one stage looks nothing like the next. A butterfly starts life as an egg from which a caterpillar hatches. The caterpillar eats and grows until it changes into a chrysalis with a hard skin. Inside this skin the chrysalis changes again, and out comes a butterfly.

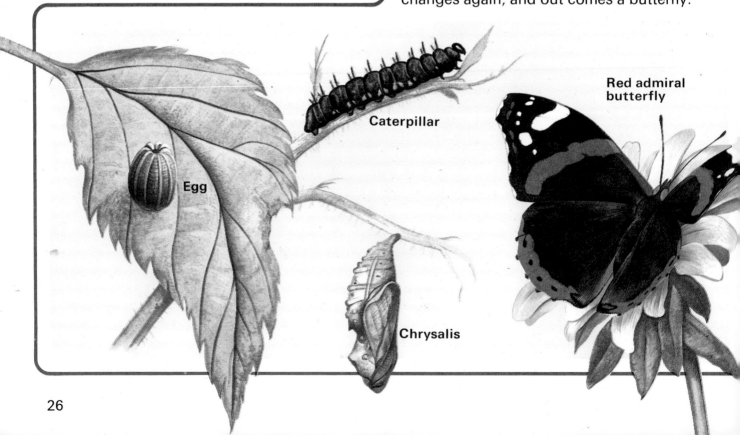

Egg

Caterpillar

Chrysalis

Red admiral butterfly

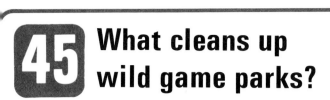

45 What cleans up wild game parks?

In countries where there are still lots of wild animals, there are usually protected areas of land for wildlife to live in called game parks, or reservations. Some African game parks are roamed by African elephants and the black and white rhinos. Large herds of antelope still move across the African plains, well away from the new cities.

You might suppose that all these wild animals make an awful lot of dung, yet the game parks do not get littered with the stuff. In fact, dung is not often seen in the game parks. So what exactly happens to it? One of the main answers is given by the picture. Dung beetles quickly roll up the dung and bury it as food for themselves and their grubs.

46 What lives inside a bubble?

Of the many kinds of spiders there is only one that lives all its life in water. The water spider is like other spiders in that it breathes air, so to live underwater it has to take air down with it. It carries air under water in the form of a bubble. Or rather bubbles, because it uses many small bubbles to make its large underwater bubble nest, or air bell.

To make its nest the water spider first spins some silk thread underwater, usually attaching it to a water weed. Then it rises to the surface and jerks its back legs so as to trap a small bubble of air against the underside of its hairy abdomen, or rear part. Then it swims down again to the bit of spun silk and attaches the air bubble to it.

This clever procedure is repeated many times and every time the spider adds another small bubble. Each one combines with those already attached to make a larger and larger bubble. Whenever necessary, the spider spins another length of silk to keep its air bell in the exact position it has chosen.

When its air bell home is finished, the water spider then gets inside it. This does not make the air bell break up because it is held firmly together by its silken net. The spider then waits for some water insect or other small swimmer to pass by, or to bump into one of the silk strands stretching from the nest. The moment this happens, the spider dashes out from its air bell to trap the unsuspecting victim, which it then hauls back to its bubble nest to eat in comfort.

47 What do koalas use for food?

Koalas live up gum trees in Australia. They climb a tree in a series of short, four-legged hops, sometimes, as the picture shows, with a baby koala clinging on too.

A koala spends nearly all of its time in the gum trees. Its only true food is the tender leaves of these eucalyptus trees, although it may go down to the ground every now and then to lick soil. In the same way that a bird eats grit, the soil helps the koala with its digestion. In fact, koalas are very choosey. Not only do they eat just eucalyptus leaves, but only those of the local region, and where many trees have been felled, koalas starve.

48 How dangerous is a gorilla?

King Kong and later Hollywood thrillers gave us the idea that all gorillas were savage monsters, just as Tarzan films gave us the idea that all chimpanzees were clowns. In the last 20 years, much more attention has been paid to these great apes, our nearest relatives, in their natural homes. It seems that far from being a dangerously savage beast, the gorilla is a surprisingly gentle animal. As for a sense of humour, we know that both chimps and gorillas have one because they, like us, are very intelligent animals.

Gorillas live in the rain forests of central Africa where they have become rare, partly as a result of being hunted by people. They wander through the jungle in groups of one fully-grown male together with his wives and children. The gorilla group eats vegetable and fruit food only, and is never known to attack people unless badly provoked. Even then, only the male will attack and he will try to scare you away first, with a noisy show of breast-beating and rushing sideways.

49 Which animal travels furthest?

This record must go to a slender, graceful seabird about 35 centimetres long called the Arctic tern. This is the champion of all animal travellers because it makes the longest regular migration in the world – between the poles.

Its immense return journey of more than ·35,000 kilometres allows the Arctic tern to enjoy the short summers both of the Arctic and of the Antarctic regions. The rest of the year the Arctic tern spends in flight, winging its way over lonely expanses of ocean, sometimes descending to the surface to catch small fishes or other sea foods. As its name shows, it nests in very northerly regions.

50 Which animal is the best engineer?

This time the prize goes to the beaver, which is a rodent, a relative of rats and mice, but is much bigger at about one metre long. The beaver lives in northern parts of the world, mainly in Canada, Scandinavia and Russia. It spends most of its time in rivers where it builds the family homes, or beaver dams, that have become so famous.

The beaver is an excellent swimmer, having webbed hind feet, a powerful, rudder-like tail and dense, oily fur that keeps out cold and wet. To start building, the beaver first uses a piece of its engineering equipment – its chisel-like teeth. With these, it can fell even quite large trees by gnawing them through near the base.

Not only this, but the beaver fells a tree so that it falls towards, or into, the water, so helping to make the beaver dams. The actual beaver house, or lodge, is a cone-shaped heap of sticks and mud with inner living quarters, safe underwater entrances and even a chimney to let in fresh air!

Animal Word Games

Here is a series of word games—these should be completed before playing the **Name Game** . . . they will help!

There are 6 word games with words hidden in them. Each game has a list of clues. The answers will be the names of any of the creatures mentioned in this book.

All you have to do is find the answer in the word game by joining up the letters in a horizontal (left or right) and vertical (up or down) pattern, starting with the first letter of the answer. A single letter may be used in more than one word – some answers have more than one word!

EXAMPLE

Answers
STARLING
RABBIT

Note: the A and R are used in both words.

R.	L	I
A	B	N
T	B	G.
S	I	T

WORD GAME 1

```
N G U L W
I O D L O
R R E H A
R A I K L
P I R O A
```

1 This creature lives in large towns (7,3)
2 Displays a red spot (7,4)
3 The most silent of birds (3)
4 Eats eucalyptus leaves (5)

WORD GAME 2

```
I H C E T
D I N R C
N L O E I
A N G L T
P E A R C
```

1 Has long spines and waddles (7)
2 A flesh-eating bird (5)
3 Has scales and a long tail (8)
4 A great migrator (6,4)

WORD GAME 3

```
A T X E B
L Y O E Y
P P F L E
L U E A N
B S W H O
```

1 Has a beak, webbed feet and a flat tail (8)
2 Feeds on krill (4,5)
3 Carries shopping baskets (5,3)
4 Dustbin robber (3)

WORD GAME 4

```
N O T N A
E I L L L
L R M I R
O A T G O
P D P A N
```

1 A sort of grouse (9)
2 It lives in rain forests (7)
3 Can change with iodine (7)
4 Makes traps (3-4)

WORD GAME 5

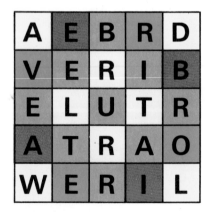

1 Has long narrow toes (5,4)
2 Punches holes in leaves (6,4)
3 Lives in the ocean, lays eggs on land (6)
4 Has oily fur that keeps out the cold and wet (6)

WORD GAME 6

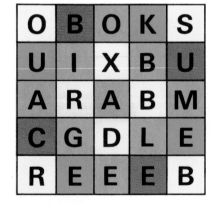

1 It might live in a mousehole (6,3)
2 Doesn't mind the prickles (6)
3 Never needs a shelter (4,2)
4 Doesn't like flies (7)

The Animal Name Game

GO

Top row: A J S P R Z T K P W V D

Left column: A E L M I O B F L N G C

Right column: D C R S A G I E B L Q U

Bottom row: C A H N E D O R T Y X U

The Animal Name Game

You will need a dice, coloured counters, pencil and paper. The players take turns in throwing the dice and moving their counters. Starting at 'GO' you throw the dice and move your counter along the outer circle of squares by the number thrown. You then write down the letter shown in the square you have landed on. When you have enough letters to form the name of any creature mentioned in this book, you write the name out and cross the letters used off your list. You can then put a counter on one of the squares of the centre box.

The aim is to complete a line of 5 counters (vertical, horizontal or diagonal) in the centre box. You may block your opponent's line with one of your counters, but you may then find it more difficult to complete a line yourself. A player may use any creature's name only once, the other player(s) may also use that name—but only once. Some of the names will be found in the **Word Games** on the previous page.

The game may also be played so that the winner is the first to cover a block of 6 squares. Or simply carry on the game until all the squares in the centre box have been filled— then the player with the most counters is the winner.

INDEX